SandCastle

Rhyme Time

Elaine's Rain Cane

Anders Hanson

Consulting Editor, Diane Craig, M.A./Reading Specialist

Publishing Company

Published by ABDO Publishing Company, 4940 Viking Drive, Edina, Minnesota 55435.

Printed in the United States.

Credits
Edited by: Pam Price
Curriculum Coordinator: Nancy Tuminelly
Cover and Interior Design and Production: Mighty Media
Photo and Illustration Credits: BananaStock Ltd., Brand X Pictures, Comstock, Corbis Images, Hemera, Tracy Kompelien, PhotoDisc, Stockbyte

Library of Congress Cataloging-in-Publication Data

Hanson, Anders, 1980-
    Elaine's rain cane / Anders Hanson.
       p. cm. -- (Rhyme time)
    Includes index.
    ISBN 1-59197-788-6 (hardcover)
    ISBN 1-59197-894-7 (paperback)
    1. English language--Rhyme--Juvenile literature. I. Title. II. Rhyme time (ABDO Publishing Company)

PE1517.H37 2004
428.1'3--dc22
                                                                    2004049513

SandCastle™ books are created by a professional team of educators, reading specialists, and content developers around five essential components that include phonemic awareness, phonics, vocabulary, text comprehension, and fluency. All books are written, reviewed, and leveled for guided reading, early intervention reading, and Accelerated Reader® programs and designed for use in shared, guided, and independent reading and writing activities to support a balanced approach to literacy instruction.

Let Us Know

After reading the book, SandCastle would like you to tell us your stories about reading. What is your favorite page? Was there something hard that you needed help with? Share the ups and downs of learning to read. We want to hear from you! To get posted on the ABDO Publishing Company Web site, send us e-mail at:

sandcastle@abdopub.com

SandCastle Level: Fluent

Words that rhyme do not have to be spelled the same. These words rhyme with each other:

brain

main

cane

pane

chain

plane

drain

rain

lane

vein

Patrick uses a **cane** fishing pole when he goes fishing with his grandpa.

Henry uses his **brain** when he studies.

Kim rides her bike down
the **lane**.

Kevin's dad helps him fix the **chain** on his bike.

Denise peers through the **pane** of glass.

Amy is taking a bath.

When she is done, the water will go down the **drain**.

Isaac plays with a toy plane.

Rachel's family just bought a new house on **Main** Street.

It is easy to see every **vein** in this leaf because it is so big.

Carrie likes to walk in the **rain**.

Elaine's Rain Cane

Elaine has a magical rain cane.
With one wave of this cane,
Elaine makes the clouds drain
all the rain they contain.

15

This cane was not easy to obtain.
She had to take a plane to Spain.

While walking down a lane,
she saw it through the pane
of a store called The Magician's Brain.

Elaine could not refrain.
She had to buy the magic cane.

18

On her way home from Spain,
she met a farmer named Shane.

19

Shane was feeling a strain because his crops would not grow in the dry terrain.

Elaine waved her cane, and it began to rain.

Shane smiled as his crops grew in the rain.

He no longer felt the strain.

21

Rhyming Riddle

What do you call the largest path?

Main lane

Glossary

cane. the strong, flexible stem of a grass such as sugarcane or bamboo; a walking stick

pane. a framed sheet of glass set into a window or door

refrain. to prevent oneself from doing something

strain. excessive stress or demand on one's body, mind, or resources

terrain. an area of land or the physical features of an area of land

vein. a tube that carries body fluids, such as blood in a human or sap in a leaf

About SandCastle™

A professional team of educators, reading specialists, and content developers created the SandCastle™ series to support young readers as they develop reading skills and strategies and increase their general knowledge. The SandCastle™ series has four levels that correspond to early literacy development in young children. The levels are provided to help teachers and parents select the appropriate books for young readers.

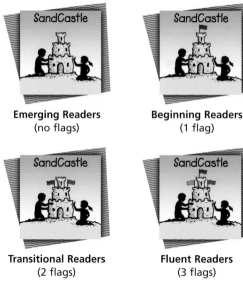

Emerging Readers
(no flags)

Beginning Readers
(1 flag)

Transitional Readers
(2 flags)

Fluent Readers
(3 flags)

These levels are meant only as a guide. All levels are subject to change.

ABDO
Publishing Company

To see a complete list of SandCastle™ books and other nonfiction titles from ABDO Publishing Company, visit **www.abdopub.com** or contact us at:
4940 Viking Drive, Edina, Minnesota 55435 • 1-800-800-1312 • fax: 1-952-831-1632